Big Bear & Little Bear
A Cautionary Tale of
Bipolar Disorder for Adults

Big Bear

WARNING

Although this book has a deceptively childlike title and is written in a literary style reminiscent of A. A. Milne, it contains descriptions of manic and depressive behaviors consistent with bipolar disorder, and discusses homosexual relationships and lifestyles.

THIS IS NOT A BOOK INTENDED FOR CHILDREN AND SHOULD NOT BE MISTAKEN FOR ONE.

CONTENTS

ACKNOWLEDGMENTS

Big Bear would like to thank his therapist for encouraging him to reach a catharsis through writing about his experience.

1 - PROLOGUE

This book does not have a happy ending. Do not look for or expect to find one.

For a brief time it almost had one; but the same factors that led to the event described in this book would resurface many years after the first writings were completed. This will be explained in the final chapter.

All of the events described in this book actually occurred; they have been highly fictionalized. In an effort to try to begin to understand or even come to terms with what happened to him, the author chose to write about this event in third person, using a simple literary style as a coping mechanism.

The arguments are real; they were written down word-for-word almost as soon as they were over. Any reader who has had to deal with someone with bipolar disorder will recognize the patterns and the cadences in them. The locales are also real – sometimes lightly and humorously encoded; no doubt many readers will de-code that 'The Provincial Little Town at the End of the World' is Provincetown, MA out on the tip of Cape Cod, a popular gay vacation spot. The names have been changed to protect all those involved, especially Little Bear.

2 - THE MEETING OF THE BEARS

Little Bear was all alone in the world. For many, many years he had lived with a different Big Bear but even in the best of circumstances things happen, sometimes without warning or without explanation. After many, many years, Little Bear parted from his Big Bear. Sometimes Love fades.

Big Bear was all alone in the world, too. Once upon a time, he had his own Big Bear. They were together many years, but sometimes nature makes its own plans and his Big Bear was laid to rest. Big Bear carried those memories deep inside him. Sometimes Love never dies.

A few years later, Big Bear and Little Bear met by chance at a Bear Event. There were many bears of many different types there. Some bears were very, very handsome; some bears were plain; all of them were looking for adventures. Big Bear was walking around looking confused by the other bears and their activities. Sometimes Love has nothing to do with it.

Little Bear followed Big Bear around for a while, looking to see what Big Bear might do. Big Bear kept walking around and around doing nothing while bears around him were playing together. Big Bear did not join in their fun. Finally, Little Bear walked up to Big Bear and said: "Hi, I'm Little Bear. Who are you?"

"I'm Big Bear," Big Bear replied, "and I'm not exactly sure why I am here. It's almost my birthday, and I heard that Bears come here to meet each other. I decided to try a Bear Event at least once before I get any older."

"And are you having any fun?" asked Little Bear.

"I feel so out of place here," Big Bear replied "everyone is just prowling around looking for fun, and I don't know anyone here."

"Well, you met me," Little Bear replied "so now you know someone. Why don't we walk around together and see what we find?"

Big Bear was a little skeptical, but some bears are very friendly and outgoing, so Little Bear and Big Bear walked around to see what the other bears were doing. Some bears were very, very friendly and popular; other bears had snooty attitudes. If they didn't like your fur, they wouldn't even talk to you. There were Wolves and Otters at the Bear Event; other species find Bears attractive, too. There were even creatures without fur there, all hoping some bear would give them a big bear hug. Big Bear was overwhelmed by most of it.

"I've always known this existed," he said "but I was never a part of it."

Little Bear and Big Bear went off by themselves for a while until the announcement that the buffet was being served brought everyone together to have some food. Bears with food in their tummies are a friendly lot. Everyone sat around snacking and watching the movie on a big screen television and talking together. Big Bear felt better about being there.

"Why don't we separate for a while, and see if we hook up again later," said Little Bear.

So Big Bear and Little Bear went off in different directions. Big Bear went to the play areas and found others bears, which, like him, were alone and wanted to make new friends. It was all new to Big Bear and he found it very exciting because it was so different. Unlike the bear watering holes with too much smoke and too much loud music, this was a new game of a different sort. Soon after, Big Bear found Little Bear again.

"So, are you enjoying yourself any more now?" asked Little Bear.

"Well, I'm not as frightened of the whole thing the way I was when I walked in" replied Big Bear.

Little Bear and Big Bear went off by themselves again. Soon they were talking like old buddies and exchanged phone numbers and email addresses. They decided to try to spend some time together as soon as they could even though they lived miles and miles away from each other. A new relationship had begun.

~

Little Bear was the oldest child in his family. His family was well off and he attended schools and went places many people could only dream about. He went to a very, very important college and earned his degree in music. There were beautiful white mountains nearby calling to him, and Little Bear soon found himself teaching at a college, and became an 'artist in residence.' On the surface, Life was good for Little Bear. He played piano, taught students, and gave concerts.

Big Bear was the fourth of five cubs in his family. Living in Middle America and having five children made things difficult at times for his family. Big Bear and his little brother never attended college. Big Bear did not have the determination to see something through if it did not interest him. Nature had taken his two oldest siblings from him, and because of this Big Bear was always sad. On the surface, Life was only tolerable for Big Bear. He lived his life for the moment, hoping that beauty and loving kindness would care for him. When he lost his Big Bear, Big Bear felt that Love died with him.

Appearances can be deceiving; for all the good things that Little Bear had acquired, there were dragons running through his brain and they needed to be kept quiet. For all of the hardships Big Bear had endured there was within him a capacity for caring if the right someone came along. For years Little Bear was able to keep his dragons quiet and Big Bear was able to care for others but not love them. No one ever saw what they had hidden inside of them.

Big Bear and Little Bear would try to see each other whenever they could. They had very diverse schedules, and sometimes this made things very easy and at other times made things nearly impossible for them. Because Little Bear taught at a school and had summertime off, he was free to visit almost any time. Big Bear had a very rigid work schedule and try as he might sometimes it was almost impossible to see Little Bear. Big Bear also shared a cave with two other bears that had even worse schedules than he, and sometimes with Little Bear there, personalities would not always be complimentary. Big Bear and Little Bear spent as much time away from Big Bear's cave as they could when Little Bear came to visit. Luckily for them, when Big Bear would go to the white mountains to visit, there would be no one to bother them, but Big Bear almost always had to travel at inopportune times because he could not change his work schedule.

Little Bear and Big Bear tried to make the most of it.

One summer Little Bear had to perform music auditions that were very, very important. Because it was important to practice, Big Bear stayed out of Little Bear's way. Little Bear practiced and practiced by himself. One day Little Bear asked Big Bear to come to the white mountains and hear his final practice. Little Bear played several pieces, all beautifully performed. Although Big Bear loved music, he knew that even if he had practiced for two lifetimes that he would never be able to create such beauty. When he was finished, Little Bear suddenly said, "I have one more piece to play, and I dedicate this to you, Big Bear, because you supported me during this hard time." Little Bear played Debussy's "Reflections on the Water" for Big Bear. Big Bear was so overtaken by the beauty of Little Bear's playing that when the music was finished, Big Bear cried and cried. "No matter what happens," he said "I will always remember you playing this piece for me."

Big Bear's talents were very diverse. Big Bear was very creative, but he knew that creativity is a fleeting thing and doesn't pay the bills. For many years he used his paws and sewed and designed things for others to wear. He even had a brief stint in professional theatre as a costumer, but after many years realized his life was bring lived running from one show to the next in rapid succession, and no one leaves a theatre humming the costumes. He also went through a succession of jobs, working hard at each one until he became so bored with what he was doing that he would go to work for something entirely new to get away from it. All that Big Bear really wanted was Empowerment over the sadness in his life, and it eluded him.

Big Bear and Little Bear would go many places together. When they did, they always wore hats that said 'BEAR" on them, or had bear paws on them. This was silly because everyone <u>knew</u> they were bears! It was not as though they had to advertise. Everyone knows who the bears are! They laughed to themselves because they knew it was silly, too.

Silly bears!

Every now and then Big Bear and Little Bear would get into an argument.

"Oh, Yeah? That's because you're a silly bear!"

"I'm a silly bear? No- YOU'RE a silly bear!"

"I'm not a silly bear - YOU'RE the really silly bear!"

Sometimes Bears who care about each other argue in silly ways so they don't hurt each other. After an argument like this, they would both end up laughing and hugging each other, because no one likes an argument.

Silly bears.

Still, sometimes they would run into difficulties. One day, Little Bear announced that he had heard a place nearby that sounded very interesting. It was an area by a river full of rocks with many pools to swim in. It was supposed to be very private if you knew which pool to go to. Since bears are covered in fur, they do not need to wear swimsuits. It was located somewhere in the green mountains west of the white mountains. With no idea exactly where they were going, Little Bear and Big Bear set out to have an adventure, guessing which direction they were supposed to be travelling in. They made many guesses and had many false starts. How can you ask someone to direct you when you have no idea where you are going?

Luckily, in the green mountains there are many places to go swimming, some of them close to the road. All you have to do is look for a lot of cars parked on the shoulder. Finally, after stopping and starting Little Bear & Big Bear came to a bridge with lots of cars. They decide to try it. The river was full of mommies and little children! Not a place for nekkid bears! They were stumped and didn't know what to do. Soon, they saw two wolves with backpacks coming down a road that went up the side of a green mountain. Figuring they had nothing to lose, they decided to be brave and ask the wolves if there were any places for men to go swimming on this river full of rocks.

"Oh, yes," replied the wolves "But you have to walk until you think you've past it, and go further than that. There are at least three swimming holes before you get to the men's swimming hole." Little Bear and Big Bear thanked the wolves and started out to seek the place Little Bear had heard about. It was a very strange path; in some spots it was so big you could have driven a car down it; in some spots the path crept around huge boulders and was no wider than a bear's paw. They walked and walked past two swimming holes full of families and adolescents swinging off a cliff on a rope. They kept walking, and the path came to an abrupt stop. "Well," said Big Bear," I wonder if this place really exists, of if those two wolves were telling us a story?"

"Well, there are some swimmers over here," said Little Bear pointing to the right, "We could ask them." Little Bear and Big Bear dropped everything and went in the water. It was very cold. Soon they came out of the water to let the sun dry them off and warm them up. They talked to the other swimmers. "Oh," said an otter, "there is a place with a sandy beach further up the river where a lot of men go. But you have to know where the path is, or you have to walk up in the river itself."

Getting some directions, Little Bear and Big Bear went back to the spot where they had come to the abrupt stop. Barely noticeable was a small flat area on the left that went up the side of the cliff. They decided to try it, and found another pathway. They walked and saw a sandy beach, complete with nekkid swimmers sunning themselves. Little Bear and Big Bear knew they had found The Secret Spot and said that they would return the next day with lunch to find a good spot to sun themselves. And they did.

The second time the path made complete sense to them and they found The Secret Spot right away. It turned out that not only was there a sandy beach, but a large rocky ledge as well! Previous swimmers had built small stone monoliths and standing stone piles out of the many rocks in the river. It was a sunny day and they enjoyed themselves, swimming and lying nekkid in the sun, and having a good time.

Then they noticed something.

Next to one side of the river was a leafy wood with many trails, and sometimes one of the swimmers would take a walk into the woods. Big Bear decided to check out what was going on. Soon, Big Bear found out that he was in the 100 Pecker Wood. It turned out that there were many, many paths in the 100 Pecker Wood. Some of them went through sunny fields, some of them went along the edges of the river, and many of them led deeper into the 100 Pecker Wood. Big Bear was amazed at what he had discovered and went to tell Little Bear what he had found. Soon, the two of them were up and about, discovering where the many paths could go. It turned out the 100 Pecker Wood was far from unoccupied. Many creatures were walking the trails. "Aha!" said Little Bear "At least we now know why this spot is so far from the road, and yet is very, very popular."

Big Bear and Little Bear made many visits to The Secret Spot and to the 100 Pecker Wood. Unfortunately, sometimes The Green-eyed Monster also visited the wood. Big Bear liked to hike the trails alone, to see what he could see. Some places in the wood were wild and uninhibited. Big Bear liked to be a solo act. Little Bear liked to tag along, mostly because he did not like walking in the wood alone. This difference in exploration styles led to some unhappy moments. In Little Bear's opinion, Big Bear enjoyed himself far too much. He felt that they should place limits on the time spent in the 100 Pecker Wood. In Big Bear's opinion, Little Bear needed to trust him more. Sometimes he felt Little Bear intruded on his fun. It was not a conflict easily to be solved. In the end, they would wear watches if they ventured into the 100 Pecker Wood and announce at what time they would be returning to the beach. This is how they did not solve the conflict, but at least had ground rules they would both agree to.

Big Bear and Little Bear continued their adventures whenever they could. Once they decided to go to the Provincial Little Town at the End of the World for a Halloween weekend. They stayed at a hotel with lots of other bears and had a grand time, going to the very top of a tall stone monument, shopping in the many little shops, and going to eat in the small restaurants. They brought costumes and on Halloween night everyone in the town dressed up and walked the streets, taking pictures of everyone's costumes, visiting the watering holes, acting silly, and going out for slices of pizza when the night was through. It was so much fun that Big Bear and Little Bear agreed that they would do it again every year.

One day Little Bear came for a visit and was very, very serious. "I have something important to tell you," he said, "especially now that we are becoming good friends." "What's the matter?" asked Big Bear. "A long time ago," he began, "I was very, very sick. Dragons were running through my brain, and they made me do and say horrible things. I ended up in a hospital for a long, long time. There they gave me many, many pills until the dragons stopped running around and were quiet again. Every day I have to take these pills to keep the dragons asleep. You see, I am bipolar."

Big Bear did not understand; he thought Little Bear was trying to be funny. "What are you telling me?" he asked. "What are you telling me? That you are a <u>bipolar bear</u>?" Big Bear rolled on the floor, laughing. He did not mean to be insensitive; he just did not understand.

"I am being serious, Big Bear," Little Bear continued, "Being bipolar is a hard, hard thing to deal with. You are happy one minute and crying the next. Everything is fine and then, without warning, suddenly you are mad at everyone and everything! Sometimes you sit there and cry; sometimes you are so wound up that you feel like you can climb the walls! Sometimes things get so bad that the only thing that can happen is to go back to the hospital until the dragons stop. The hospitalization is a horrible thing to go through, almost worse than the dragons themselves."

Big Bear stopped laughing; he knew something important was being discussed. "I'm sorry I laughed at you, Little Bear," he said "but you have to admit that being called a bipolar bear does sound funny, like a character in a television show. How often do you have to take your medications?"

"I have to take them every single day," replied Little Bear, "every morning and every night ... forever."

Big Bear hugged Little Bear. "I'm so sorry I was laughing at you, Little Bear," he said, "I thought you were trying to be funny." Little Bear hugged him back and said "That's because you're a silly bear!"

Big Bear and Little Bear continued to develop their friendship. Since there was never a sign of Little Bear's dragons, Big Bear soon forgot that the conversation ever took place. Little Bear continued to take his medications every day and night.

One day Big Bear announced to Little Bear that he wanted to do something special and that he was going to make pasta for Little Bear, who was curious, since for most bears that meant going and buying a box of pasta at a grocery store. "NO!" said Big Bear "Not dry, boxed stuff! I am going to make you *fresh* pasta!"

"Oh," said Little Bear "Do you have a pasta-making machine?" Big Bear took a deep breath. "I have a machine," he began "that will cut the finished pasta for you, but it does not mix the dough or anything else. Some things a bear has to do for himself." Big Bear and Little Bear took a trip to the supermarket and Big Bear bought two kinds of flour and fresh eggs. When they got home Big Bear showed Little Bear how his Mamma bear made pasta. Big Bear had a great time mixing the eggs with flour and water and kneading and kneading the dough into a smooth ball. "Now" he said "we take a piece of dough and put it through the rollers two or three times until it gets to be nice and smooth. Then we put it through the cutter and strips of pasta come out the other side. Your job, Little Bear, is to separate the pasta strips on this rack so that they can dry for a little while."

Big Bear put the smooth pasta through the cutters and turned the crank. Little Bear took the cut pasta and hung it to dry. Soon they had lots and lots of pasta strips hanging in the kitchen. When all the pasta was cut, Big Bear started to clean up and Little Bear started to boil the water. Soon they had all the fixings for a nice supper and sat down to eat it.

"What do you think of the pasta we made?" asked Big Bear while they were eating. "This is so good," Little

Bear said, "I have never made my own pasta before, and no one ever made me pasta from scratch. Thank you, Big Bear."

"You are welcome" replied Big Bear.

One weekend Big Bear went up to see Little Bear at his school. Little Bear showed him around, showing him Little Bear's office, his different classrooms, and the big auditorium where plays were presented. "This is what I really want to show you," said Little Bear as he brought Big Bear through two heavy doors, "This is the Recital Hall where the music students give concerts." Little Bear led Big Bear through the hall. There were many seats and a stage at one end. On the stage was a nine-foot grand piano with the top open. "Wow!" said Big Bear "It's amazing to get to see one of these pianos up close." Little Bear sat at the keyboard and played a few chords. "Yes," he said "This is a beautiful piano and it is in fine tune...and I have a surprise for you," he said with a wicked smile. Little Bear pulled a handful of music books out of his briefcase. "Since it's late and no one else is around in the building, I thought you might want to sing some songs."

"You are a really silly Bear," laughed Big Bear.

"Yes. That is why you love me," said Little Bear opening one of the books. "Do you want to start with

Jerome Kern or Cole Porter?"

With no one around to hear them, Little Bear played song after song and Big Bear stood center stage and sang his big bruin heart out. It was a wonderful, wonderful hour. Finally, they ran out of music.

"Thank you so much!" said Big Bear with tears in his eyes, "It's been a long, long time since anyone has wanted to hear me sing."

"Anytime," replied Little Bear.

~

Soon the summertime ended and the weather started turning into autumn. "It is getting close to Halloween" Big Bear said one day. "Are we going to go to the Provincial Little Town at the End of the World again this year?" "Oh, yes!" said Little Bear, "We had such a good time there last year! What shall we do for costumes this year?"

Big Bear and Little Bear worked and worked. Big Bear decided to go as a spaceman. Little Bear decided to dress up like a cartoon show bear celebrity. They packed their car and drove to the Provincial Little Town. The weather did not look promising; rain was predicted and should last for the entire weekend. The two bears hoped that the good weather would last. They drove and drove. Finally they got to their hotel and found other bears to talk to. Soon it was suppertime and everyone went to the dining room to eat and see who was new and who was there. It turned out there were many bears from All Over coming to the Provincial Little Town for Halloween. Everyone brought a costume and everyone there was looking forward to having a good time on Halloween, walking the streets and having a parade. After supper, everyone decided to go to the watering holes and see who else was in town. No one noticed the clouds were starting to get dark and thick.

Little Bear and Big Bear went into town. Many bears and other creatures were out and about. Soon, the skies turned to mist and everyone went inside to stay dry. Little Bear & Big Bear went into a watering hole. There was loud, loud music blaring and Little Bear did not like it. It was also very crowded with bears trying to stay out of the rain. Big Bear met two Biker Bears from Beantown that were very interested in talking to him. They talked and talked and got very friendly. Little Bear would not enter into the conversations. Big Bear was too busy enjoying himself to notice that Little Bear was getting very upset.

Finally, Big Bear called over to Little Bear and asked him why he wasn't joining them. "BECAUSE I DO NOT WANT TO TALK WITH THOSE BEARS!" said Little Bear in a very loud voice. Big Bear and the bears from Beantown stopped talking. "IF YOU WANT TO STAY HERE WITH THEM, THEY CAN DRIVE YOU BACK TO THE HOTEL. I AM LEAVING NOW!" Little Bear turned and stared to leave. "We are sorry, Big Bear" said the Beantown bears, "We did not realize we were making a problem for you." Big Bear went outside to find Little Bear. He knew that something was very, very wrong, not just with his talking to two strange bears, but with the whole situation. Little Bear and Big Bear drove back to their hotel without speaking to each other. It was raining very hard when they got back.

The rain continued to pour down on the town and the wind came up and blew it across the parking lot of the hotel. Big Bear & Little Bear went back to their room and took their coats off. Big Bear sat on the bed, wondering when someone was going to say something.

"Why did you talk to them?" Little Bear finally asked.

"I talk with everyone," replied Big Bear "Is that so unusual?"

"Why did you talk to THEM?" said Little Bear again.

"Are you mad because I was talking to them in particular, or because I wasn't talking to you?" asked Big Bear.

"I DIDN'T LIKE THEM!" started Little Bear all over again "WHO KNOWS where they came from or what they've done!"

"We've been down this road before," said Big Bear as calmly as he could. "We go to Bear Places to meet other bears, and when I do, you get upset about it."

"WHY WOULD YOU BE INTERESTED IN THEM?" cried Little Bear.

"I talked with them because they were friendly and we all started talking together. I tried to get you into the conversation, but you would not walk over to us," said Big Bear, still trying to keep his voice calm. "I talk to many bears wherever we go. Why is doing this such a problem now?"

The discussion started going in circles. Big Bear wanted to know exactly what he had done that made Little Bear so angry with him. Little Bear talked and talked in circles and never told Big Bear exactly what set his mood off. Finally it got so tiring that they turned off the lights to try to go to sleep. Neither Big Bear nor Little Bear went to sleep.

After a long time of lying there in the darkness, Little Bear said: "It doesn't matter to me if you talk to other bears."

"WHAT?" screamed Big Bear, sitting up in bed, "That is the most ironic thing I've heard all night! First you start screaming at me in public for talking to other bears and now you are telling me that it DOESN'T MATTER? What is going on here?"

"I'm not staying," yelled Little Bear, getting out of bed and going for his clothes, "I'm getting out of here now!"

"And what are you going to do?" demanded Big Bear. 'What are you going to do? Knock on one of our friend's doors and see if you can share their room? Go to sleep out in the car? Or are you just going to drive home and leave me here? It's three o'clock in the morning!"

"I CAN'T STAY HERE!" shouted Little Bear "I have to get out!"

"If you leave me here," said Big Bear calmly, "It's all over."

Little Bear stopped trying to pack his things and climbed back into bed. Big Bear rolled over and put his arm around him, but he knew something was still horribly, horribly wrong.

The next morning was cold and damp. The rain never stopped and it constantly blew through the Provincial Little Town in sheets, soaking anyone who ventured outdoors. Although Big Bear & Little Bear went down to breakfast with the other bears, Big Bear felt very, very cold and his body ached, so when they came back from breakfast, he climbed into bed, and pulled the covers up. Little Bear turned on the television and watched some shows. Neither of them talked very much. Big Bear finally fell asleep. When he awoke, Little Bear was lying on the bed next to him. "It's almost time for the party at the watering hole. Do you want to go and mix with the other Bear Clubs?" he asked.

"No," said Big Bear "I really feel too cold to go outside and get soaked. I also do not want a repeat of last night's argument."

"How about supper?" asked Little Bear "Do you still want to go to that?"

"Sure," said Big Bear "We can still eat supper and then decide if we will still do Halloween, since the rains have not stopped. I want to sleep some more, though."

Little Bear let Big Bear sleep some more, and woke him when it was almost time to leave for supper. The two of them drove through pouring rain to find the little restaurant. It was a little restaurant full of big bears! Everyone squeezed themselves in and had a nice meal. Big Bear and Little Bear enjoyed talking with everyone there. Soon, they drove back to the hotel, for even though it was still raining, it was Halloween night. When they got back to their room, Little Bear asked, "Well, Big Bear - what shall we do about Halloween?"

"Let's wear our costumes down to the party in the hotel," he said, "But I do not want to walk around in Town in the rain and get my costume all wet."

So that is what they did. Big Bear and Little Bear got all dressed up and went to the dining room of the hotel. Many bears were there and many had made special costumes just for the party. There were Vikings and warriors and scary monsters. Everyone walked around and took pictures. Everyone watched the rain still coming down. It seemed as if the weather was not going to cooperate. Finally, someone said that they were going into town, but not in costume, and most everyone agreed that it seemed like the practical thing to do. Big Bear and Little Bear went back to their room to take their costumes off. "Do you want to go into town?" asked Little Bear. "Sure," Big Bear replied, "We drove all the way out here to the Provincial Little Town at the End of the World, so we might try to enjoy what's left of this weekend.

Big Bear and Little Bear drove into town and found a place to park. The heavy rains had stopped, but it was still misting out. That did still not stop a lot of people from walking through the streets in costume showing off. The two of them walked around, laughing at the costumes and talking some pictures. Finally they went to a very spirited pizza shop and fit themselves inside and ordered slices of pizza. It was very, very crowded inside. People in costume kept coming in and out to buy slices of pizza. No one paid any attention to the two bears sitting at a table with their pizza.

"I'm sorry I acted the way I did," said Little Bear.

"I'm sorry this weekend turned out the way it did," said Big Bear "We waited a long time to come here, and it turned into such a horrible time."

"Maybe tomorrow will be a happier day," said Little Bear.

The next day the sun came out bright and clear. The strong wind blew the clouds away as everyone finished breakfast and packed their belongings into their cars.

"Isn't that always the way!" said one of the bears.

Big Bear and Little Bear decided to go into town and do some shopping now that the weather was so clear. They took a friend with them and went into shop after shop looking for bargains. They stopped and took pictures in front of one house with unusual sculptures in front of it. They met many people they had seen the day before. Everyone wanted to go shopping now that the rains had stopped. They bumped into the two bears from Beantown. Everyone talked about how nice it was now that the sun had come out.

Big Bear, Little Bear, and their friend bought many, many things up and down the street, and made trips back to the car. Finally, it started to get later in the afternoon. Big Bear and Little Bear decided to eat supper in town, but their friend had a long trip home and decided to leave. They decided to eat at a restaurant with lobster pots in front of it. For some reason, they were able to get a table in front of a large window where they could watch the setting sun. They had a wonderful meal, eating and watching the sky turn from blue into yellow and start to go dark.

"I'm sorry," they both said at the same time.

They drove to Big Bear's home, and the next morning Little Bear left for the white mountains.

It was another two weeks before they could see each other again. Little Bear was very, very busy at school doing classes, teaching lessons, and preparing for concerts. He was running around at all hours every single day to make sure he got everything done. Big Bear went back to work, working almost every night until very late. Soon, the only time Big Bear and Little Bear had for talking was on their computers during lunchtime, or very late at night. During their second week apart Big Bear started to notice something strange was starting to happen every time the two of them talked: Little Bear started cutting the letters shorter and shorter. Soon, as soon as Big Bear signed on and typed 'Hello. How are you?' Little Bear was excusing himself to run back to classes. One day Little Bear sent Big Bear a message to be online at a certain time so that they could talk. Big Bear signed himself on early and waited for 'Little Bear' to appear in his 'Bear Buddy List.' As soon as he saw 'Little Bear' sign on, Big Bear sent him a message. Little Bear sent back a short reply "I can't talk now. Bye." Big Bear started to become very upset by all of this. Why would Little Bear ask him to wait, and then not want to talk to him?

A couple of days later, Big Bear was online and saw 'Little Bear' appear on his 'Bear Buddy List.' He decided to ask Little Bear is he was going to come to visit.

"Hello, Little Bear," he typed in. "Are you coming down this weekend?"

"WHAT'S THAT QUESTION SUPPOSED TO MEAN?" Little Bear typed back.

"That question is supposed to ask you if you are coming down to see me," replied Big Bear.

"WHY ARE YOU ASKING ME THAT WAY?" demanded Little Bear.

Big Bear was very confused. All he did was ask a question, and now little Bear was yelling at him. He decided to ask again, "Are you coming down to see me this weekend?"

"YOU DON'T WANT ME TO COME DOWN. THAT'S WHY YOU ASKED ME THAT WAY!" yelled Little Bear.

"WHAT way? What are you talking about, Little Bear?"

"You don't want me to come down! If you wanted me to come down, you'd have asked me WHEN I was coming down, not IF I was coming down! You don't want me there!"

"All I have done," replied Big Bear as calmly as he could "is ask a question that I needed an answer to. All I want to know is if you are going to come down to see me this weekend. This is not a difficult question."

"Why are you asking me to come down if you do not want me to come down?" demanded Little Bear.

"I did not say I did not want you to come down to see me - you did, Little Bear," replied Big Bear.

"THEN WHY DID YOU ASK ME THAT WAY?"

"Look - I am not going to talk in circles. I want you to come down to see me. When are you coming down to see me?" asked Big Bear.

"FRIDAY. After you get out of work." Then Little Bear signed off.

All day Friday while he was at work, Big Bear worried about what was happening to Little Bear. He started to get a very uneasy feeling in the pit of his stomach. He started worrying about what he was going to say and what was going to happen when Little Bear and he met that night.

After work, Big Bear drove to his apartment, and when he arrived, there was no Little Bear truck in front of the building. He thought that that was very odd. He went inside to see if there were any telephone messages; there were not. He sat down and waited and wondered. Finally, the phone rang; it was Little Bear.

"I got lost," said Little Bear "I am trying to get back to the highway to get to your apartment."

"How did you get lost?" asked Big Bear, "You know the way to my house."

"I don't know! I was trying a new shortcut and it didn't work. Once I get back to the highway I will get there," he said.

Little Bear did not arrive for almost another hour. It was getting to be very early in the morning by this time. Finally, Big Bear heard a car door shut in front of his house. He waited for Little Bear to come inside. There was a long pause where nothing happened. Then, the doorbell rang. Confused, Big Bear went to open the door. There was the sound of loud rock-and-roll music playing when he opened the door. Little Bear was standing there holding a stuffed figure that sang 1950s songs.

"ISN'T THIS GREAT? DON'T YOU JUST LOVE IT?" shouted Little Bear.

"Yes. But where, how ... what happened to you?" asked Big Bear.

"WHAT ARE YOU TALKING ABOUT?"

"You should have been here a long time ago. You called to say you had gotten lost. *How* did you get lost?" asked Big Bear.

"I BOUGHT THIS AT THE GAS STATION ON THE CORNER. I THOUGHT IT WAS COOL," replied Little Bear.

"Yes," replied Big Bear "It's really cute, but it's two a.m., you are going to wake the neighbors, you are late and you said you had gotten lost. What happened?"

"I DON'T KNOW."

Big Bear decided to try another route. "So, how are you doing?" he asked.

Suddenly, Little Bear started crying. "OH, IT'S AWFUL! I CAN'T STAND IT!" he started to say, tears creeping down his cheeks. "Everyone is so stupid! They want, they want, they want - and they never stop to ask me - they just tell me! They never think about me!" Little Bear was sobbing loudly by this time. "It's the end of the semester, I have so much work to do, and everyone thinks I have nothing to do except do things for them! Everyone wants me to do their work for them, especially things they do not want to do!"

"What are you talking about?"

Little Bear stood up and started pacing the room. He stopped crying and started to get angry. The more he paced the angrier he became.

"They're all JEALOUS! They hate me! No matter what I do, I never get the better students! Anyone that someone does not want to teach they shuffle off on me! They want their students to make them look good! They don't care about me! They just want me out of the department!" Little Bear was pacing furiously. "They always act so high and mighty because they have their doctorates and I don't."

"You have a degree from one of the oldest and most prestigious colleges in the country," said Big Bear, "That is hardly something to be ashamed of, or ignored."

Little Bear sat down and started to cry again. 'Don't you see," he cried, "that they are trying to get rid of me? I never get to pick my students; I get who is left after they chose the ones they want. They always take the best for themselves. They are jealous of my talents and they want to see me fail."

"What?" asked Big Bear.

"Yes," Little Bear started up again, "they are jealous and they want me to fail." Little Bear continued crying for a while. "Oh, you don't know how terrible it is," he began; "Now I know what all the talented composers were going through."

"I have no idea what you are talking about," replied Big Bear.

"You should; you did this to me, you know."

"Did <u>what</u>?"

"You did this to me! I read your book where you talk about intuition and how people are psychic. You opened my eyes."

"I did *what* to you?"

"I now know what the composers were thinking when they wrote their music! I can feel their anguish! I can feel their pain!" Little Bear started crying violently, "When I play their music, I can feel what they were thinking and how they felt! I know what they were feeling!"

Little Bear suddenly stopped crying and started pacing again. "I know what my students are thinking, too. I can feel what they think before they start talking. I know what the staff is thinking, too! That is why I know they are jealous of me!" Little Bear was pacing in circles. "They don't want me there! They keep hoping that if they make me mad enough I'll leave - they hate me so much! Why are they doing this to me? To *Me*!" Little Bear started crying all over again.

Big Bear was getting very concerned. Little Bear was acting strangely and not making any sense. He was vacillating back and forth between extremes and Big Bear was not sure what Little Bear would say or do next.

Finally, Little Bear stopped crying. Big Bear asked him if he wanted to go to sleep.

"You're lazy!" Little Bear blurted out.

"I'm <u>what</u>?"

"You're lazy!"

"It is almost three a.m. and you want to argue with me because you think I'm lazy?"

"Don't you see," said Little Bear taking a haughty tone, "that this is what I have to do all day? I have to motivate people. I have to make people who don't want to do anything to keep moving. It's what I do all day at school. I have to make my music students see that they have to keep practicing. If they don't practice they'll never be anything! They'll never get anywhere! I have to make them see that they have to keep playing!"

"I beg your pardon," said Big Bear, icily, "but I am not lazy! I wrote a book by sheer determination and worked until I found a publisher to buy it. I now have a book contract and have been paid for it. I also spent months reconstructing a play that I am now trying to get produced. These are hardly the accomplishments of a lazy person, someone that _You_ have to motivate!"

"Why did you ask me to come to see you when you didn't want me here in the first place?" demanded Little Bear. "You were talking online to someone when I came in!"

Big Bear sighed. "I was talking to my brother, if you must know. Why are you talking this way?"

"What are *you* talking about?" demanded Little Bear.

"You do this tactic every now and then. You say things, and then you try to accuse me of having said them first when in fact I didn't say them at all. I never said I did not want you here - you did - and now you are trying to make it sound like I said that I do not want you here."

Little Bear became instantly angry and upset. "I AM NOT GOING TO STAY HERE! I AM LEAVING RIGHT NOW!" he bellowed and started walking towards the door. Big Bear was suddenly very worried for Little Bear; if he was driving in a confused state like this, it was probably no wonder that he had gotten lost. If Little Bear left now, there was no telling what he might do, or where he would end up in his confusion. Big Bear thought quickly.

"NO! What are you going to do? Leave now in the middle of the night? What will you do? Drive all the way back home to the white mountains? Don't you think that might be a bad idea? You're tired and upset. Why don't you relax and try to get some sleep instead?"

Little Bear started to cry again. "Why does everybody hate me?" he asked.

"I do not hate you," said Big Bear quietly. "I'm tired, it's late, and I have to get to sleep. Are you going to come to bed?"

Little Bear sat there, crying. Big Bear did not know what to do. He did not know if he should put his arms around Little Bear or just stay away from him. Big Bear was very tired, very confused, and did not know what to do or say. He decided he should try to go to sleep, and hoped that Little Bear would follow him to bed.

Big Bear got into bed, waiting to see what would happen next. Little Bear finally came into the room and got under the comforter. He had stopped crying. Big Bear rolled over and put him arm around him. For a while everything was quiet and Big Bear hoped that whatever was troubling Little Bear was over long enough to let them get to sleep. In the course of time, Big Bear shifted his weight and rolled in the other direction. Little Bear jumped out of bed and started flinging the covers.

"What's the matter?" asked Big Bear.

"YOU DIDN'T HOLD ME LONG ENOUGH!" yelled Little Bear. "I'm not sleeping here! I have things to do!" Little Bear stomped out into the living room. Big Bear stayed in bed, worrying about what would happen next.

Soon, he heard the sound of his computer turning on. 'Oh, good," thought Big Bear, "Little Bear will go online until he gets bored or sleepy and then he will come back to bed. Perhaps I can get to sleep." But Big Bear did not sleep because he was very, very worried.

A very short time later, Little Bear flung the bedroom door open and started rummaging through his things, slamming drawers and muttering to himself. Big Bear knew he was not going to get much, if any sleep that night. "What are you doing?" he asked.

"CORRECTING PAPERS!" snapped Little Bear. "I have so much work I have to do!" Little Bear stomped out of the room and Big Bear could hear him turning his computer back on. A very short time later Little Bear was back in the room, slamming drawers again. "Could you try making a little less noise, please," asked Big Bear wearily, "I am trying to sleep."

"I HAVE WORK TO DO!" Little Bear came over to the edge of Big Bear's and pushed his face into Big Bear's face. "Don't you understand? I have to get things done!"

"I have to get to sleep!' Big Bear answered back.

"Well, this is what's wrong with us!" snapped little Bear. "We have different schedules, and your schedule does not mesh with mine. This is what is wrong with us - our schedules clash!" Little Bear slammed the door to Big Bear's room when he left.

After what seemed like an eternity of senseless

noises, Big Bear fell asleep. Soon he was woken up with a start- someone was pounding something! Big Bear got out of bed and went into the living room where Little Bear was pounding the ceiling with the broom handle.

"WHAT are you doing?" shouted Big Bear.

"The neighbors are making too much noise!" said Little Bear throwing the broom on the floor. "I am going to go upstairs and tell them to stop making such a racket!" Little Bear was about to march out the door.

"DON'T!" cautioned Big Bear. "DO NOT go upstairs and annoy my neighbors! You will cause big problems for me if you go and annoy people!" Big Bear turned to go into his room. Little Bear was right behind him, yelling again.

"I HAVE A SCHEDULE! I have to stick to my schedule! I can't have people throwing me off schedule!"

"I have a schedule, too," replied Big Bear "I have to get my sleep so that I can wake up and go to work again tomorrow. Obviously, the fact that *I* might have a schedule is of no importance to you!" Big Bear lay down on his bed, wishing this whole situation would just disappear. Big Bear cried himself to sleep.

Big Bear

3 - ALL HELL BREAKS LOOSE

When Big Bear woke up Little Bear seemed subdued. Still wondering what he would find when he got back home, Big Bear went to work for his shift, a little weary from the previous day's events. When he got home he found that Little Bear had gone out shopping and filled his refrigerator. While Big Bear was at work Little Bear called his guardian and had a long talk and they had advised him to contact his mental health physician – who was not available, so Little Bear was put in contact with his 'cover' who prescribed something to 'take the edge off' until his doctor returned. Things seemed to have calmed down somewhat.

Big Bear woke up to Little Bear screaming onto his phone: "THIS IS AN EMERGENCY! I AM HAVING A BAD REACTION TO MY MEDS!" Little Bear had called his guardian who was trying to calm him down. Big Bear started to cry; there wasn't much else left for him to do.

Little Bear finally calmed down and saw Big Bear crying. "Why are you crying?" he asked. "I am crying because I am afraid," replied Big Bear, "Afraid that the Little Bear I've known for the last 18 months is really nothing more than a medical, chemical creation, and perhaps what I am seeing now is the REAL Little Bear." "Are you afraid of me Big Bear?" asked Little Bear. "No," replied Big Bear, I am not afraid of You; I am afraid for what is becoming of Us."

Big Bear and Little Bear decided to go to a movie; it was full of wizards and flying cars and large, hairy spiders. It was a strange choice for a movie to go see. Little Bear got up and walked around several times during the movie. Big Bear wondered how long the calm was going to last.

Soon after returning home, Little Bear's calm ended.

"While you were at work I called Joe," began Little Bear, "And talked about your behavior at the barbeque last month."

"What are you talking about - and don't you think it's unfair and rude to discuss me behind my back?"

"All gay bears want is sex – and they don't care with who or when."

"And you are some sort of exception to this

sweeping indictment of mankind?"

"Why can't you stop seeing other Bears?"

"If I remember correctly, Little Bear – before you came into my life I was in a ten-year monogamous relationship that only ended when He died," stated Big Bear. "When we first started seeing each other and the subject of monogamy came up *YOU* were the one to state that YOU could never offer *ME* monogamy, and if I remember the conversation correctly you also added that You said that I could not accept monogamy."

"You can't!" exclaimed Little Bear.

"That is a contradictory statement, even for you," replied Big Bear. "We were two bears living two states apart and saw each other every two weeks or so and somehow you were expecting that this would lead to monogamy? We both knew it couldn't. We accepted that fact."

"What about the weekend you went away to spend with Cubby!"

"Let me see," began Big Bear, "You were going away to yet another 'music weekend' and I was all alone and Cubby asked me to come up for the weekend. You knew about the entire thing from the beginning – it's not like I tried to hide this from you. But you still got all bent out of shape over it – even though you stated that we could never have monogamy."

"I went to the music conference because it was work – *You were out <u>having fun</u>!*" yelled Little Bear.

"And so - as I've always suspected – you keep scorecards about which of us had more sex on a certain weekend excursion and how many playmates each of us had, and somehow when you perceive that I had more than you did I become the Bad Bear?" questioned Big Bear. "To be the Good Bear I have to have less sex than you did?"

Little Bear became instantly angry and upset. "I AM NOT GOING TO STAY HERE! I AM LEAVING RIGHT NOW!" he bellowed and started walking towards the door.

"You are starting this all over again," said Big Bear.

"Starting WHAT?" demanded Little Bear

"You are starting to bring up the same things over and over again and then you try to make it sound like I am the cause of it," said Big Bear.

"What are *you* talking about?" demanded Little Bear.

"You do this tactic every so often. You say things, and then you try to accuse me of having said them first when in fact I didn't say them at all. I never said I want you to leave here - <u>you</u> did - and now you are trying to make it sound like <u>I</u> said that I do not want you here."

"YOU'RE LYING! You want me to leave!" screamed Little Bear.

"We have been down this road too many times this weekend," said Big Bear, "it's making me very tired and very upset."

Little Bear started to cry again. "Why does everybody hate me?" he cried.

"STOP CRYING, NOW!" bellowed Big Bear, "This crying tactic is getting old!"

Little Bear was taken aback, momentarily, and stopped crying.

"So, when are you going to move in with Marco?" asked Little Bear.

"Why would I move in with Marco?" asked Big Bear.

"The last time we went to the Provincial Little Town at the End of the World you talked to him for an hour; when you said good-bye to me at the end of that trip you should have done a better job of it. I know you are going to leave me and move in with him," stated Little Bear.

"If that is what you are thinking then you have another think coming," stated Big Bear as calmly as he could, "one action does not lead to the other."

Little Bear started to cry again. "Why does everybody hate me?" he cried.

Little Bear started walking around the apartment ranting, walking, and ranting again. Big Bear became very concerned. If he called Little Bear's guardian Little Bear might become more violent, he also knew that another hospitalization would probably help Little Bear but could potentially destroy Little Bear's career. Big Bear knew he was watching Little Bear go near The Edge.

"Well, this is what's wrong with us!" snapped little Bear. "We have different schedules, and your schedule does not mesh with mine. This is what is wrong with us - our schedules clash! I HAVE A SCHEDULE! I have to stick to my schedule! I can't have people throwing me off schedule! When I play their music, I can feel what they were thinking and how they felt! I know what they were feeling! I know what my students are thinking, too. I can feel what they think before they start talking. I know what the staff is thinking, too! That is why I know they are jealous of me!" Little Bear was pacing in circles. "They don't want me there! They keep hoping that if they make me mad enough I'll leave - they hate me so much! Why are they doing this to me? To *Me*!" Little

Bear started crying all over again and started to flail his arms violently. Big Bear was compelled to go over to him to try to stop him from possibly hurting himself and finally put his arms around him.

"I HAVE A SCHEDULE! I have to stick to my schedule! I can't have people throwing me off schedule! I HAVE A SCHEDULE! I have to stick to my schedule! I can't have people throwing me off schedule! I HAVE A SCHEDULE! I have to stick to my schedule! I can't have people throwing me off schedule! I HAVE A SCHEDULE! I have to stick to my schedule! I can't have people throwing me off schedule!" Little Bear was ranting and crying and kept repeating himself - and to his horror, Big Bear watched Little Bear liquefy and melt his way out of his arms and disappear into the floor.

Big Bear

4 - ADRIFT

Big Bear fell into an uncomfortable sleep. He had never seen anyone melt and disappear before his eyes before. He rolled from side-to-side many times trying and trying to find a position to fall asleep in. It was a long time before his eyelids could feel heavy enough to stay down.

Big Bear dreamt that he was in a large pool. It was very dark. Soon his eyes adjusted to the darkness and he could see that he was in a large underground cavern. He had no idea how he had gotten there. There was nowhere to climb up to get out of the water. Big Bear floated around for a while wondering what he should do, or could do. He finally spoke. "Well, I wonder where I am?" he said, not expecting an answer.

"You are being carried on the flood of your

emotion," A Voice replied. Big Bear spun around in the darkness "Who said that?" he asked, half-afraid that he did not want to know.

"Emotions can be very unusual things," the voice continued "Sometimes our emotions carry us on a great swell and raise us up. Sometimes they help us, sometimes they hurt us."

"And what am I doing?" asked Big Bear.

"If you are not careful, you may drown in the pool of your own despair," the voice replied.

"Drown?" Big Bear asked 'What are you talking about? And who are you, anyway?"

"I am deep within you," the reply came back.

Big Bear was very confused.

"I have just been through a traumatic experience," Big Bear started to explain to the voice "I have a friend who suddenly began to act strangely. He started talking in ways I have never heard him speak before. I have just spent three horrific days with him bordering on a living hell. Things got heated and nasty and at the peak of all this, my friend melted before my eyes and disappeared into the floor! He's gone! He has just ceased to exist anymore! I don't know where he is or how to get him back. I've been through all of this, and you're telling me that I'm going to drown if I'm not careful?"

"Emotions are strange things. Sometimes they stay beneath the surface and we may not notice that they even exist. Sometimes we feel the pull of our emotions and stand firm and ignore them. Sometimes they swirl around us so strongly that we get carried away by them."

"I'm scared, and I've been hurt by someone I care about. How can I keep from being affected by that?" asked Big Bear.

"Emotions can run awry."

"And why not?" said Big Bear. "We were happy. We were not blind to the problems in our relationship - we were working on things. We want things to improve!"

"And what happened?"

"Things are all screwed up. I have no idea what went wrong."

"Why does something have to be 'wrong'?" asked the voice.

Big Bear could feel the hackles on the back of his neck start to stand up. "We have an understanding," Big Bear began, "We try to talk about things before they blow up in our faces. This had no warning signals that I can see."

"Are you looking for control?"

"NO!" snapped Big Bear. He was aware that the waters were starting to get cooler. "I am not trying to control anything! Little Bear is the one who is out of control! He is acting very strangely! I have never seen him like this! He was talking and talking and none of it was making any sense! He kept going in circles and circles and didn't stop!" Big Bear was aware that the water was now quite chilly.

"Why are you taking this so personally?"

"Personally? How ELSE can I take this!" cried Big Bear. "Little Bear kept interrupting me and saying all sorts of horrible things about me! About us! He kept twisting things! He kept accusing me of things I never did - had no intention of doing!" Big Bear had not noticed that the calm pool was now beginning to ripple. The waters were beginning to move. "I wanted to help him, but he kept on badgering me! Little Bear kept on disturbing my sleep! As soon as I would be tired enough he would come into my room and shout things at me! I didn't deserve this!" The waters of the pool were no longer calm and started to swirl slightly.

The voice continued: "Sometimes we receive things we do not deserve; sometimes there is no other way."

"NO OTHER WAY?" yelled Big Bear. "I did nothing wrong! I was there doing nothing to Little Bear and he turned on me! I was scared, I was frightened, and I didn't know what else to do!" The waters of the pool were starting to swirl more and more. "I tried to reason with him - that didn't work! I tried to be friendly with him - that didn't work! I tried to be firm with him and he told me I hated him! What was I supposed to do?" Big Bear was suddenly aware that he was fighting an obvious current under the surface of the waters.

"Your emotions are starting to carry you away," the voice calmly said.

"I did absolutely nothing wrong! All I did was 'be there' for him and he took it all out on me! I didn't deserve to be treated this way! He started yelling and complaining and it just would not stop!" The currents were starting to pull Big Bear into a circle; the circle became a whirlpool. "I don't deserve to be treated this way!"

The waters were rushing and rushing. If the voice spoke again, Big Bear could not hear it, for he was being pulled down into the pool of his despair.

~

Big Bear lay in bed waiting for sleep to come. After what seemed like an eternity, Big Bear felt his eyelids grow heavy and he fell into an uneasy sleep. As Big Bear fell asleep, he felt himself falling slowly through space. Suddenly he hit something and stopped falling. He looked up and found he was at the bottom of a shaft and above him was a blue sky. "Well," said Big Bear, "I wonder where I am now?"

"You are in the well of your Pride," came back the reply.

"My what?" asked Big Bear, getting used to speaking to disembodied voices.

"You are stuck at the bottom of the well of your Pride."

"And how did I get here?"

"You dug this well yourself, bit by bit."

"You keep calling this a 'well' - is this well going to fill with water and drown me, like the pool?" asked Big Bear.

"No. That was the pool of the depths of your despair. This is a dry well," the voice replied.

"And I dug this myself with Pride. How does being prideful put you in a hole?"

"You see," explained the voice," Pride is a curious thing. Many people can feel pride and it causes them no problems at all."

"Like taking pride in your work?" asked Big Bear.

"Exactly."

"But somehow this does not apply to the situation at hand."

"Correct."

"Are you judging me, or is this a self-fulfilling sentence?"

"That was a creative assumption on your part," said the voice. "Most people who find themselves in your predicament would not be so eloquent in expressing their frustration."

"Frustration is quite right," began Big Bear. "Last night I dreamt I was drowning in my despair. Tonight - it is still night, correct?"

"Yes," replied the voice. 'You are asleep, but the sunlight above you helps complete the analogy."

"And the analogy is...?"

"Your pride - you keep burying yourself with your pride. Instead of your pride taking you to the top of the situation, you merely dig yourself in deeper."

"So, this hole that I find myself in can get deeper?" asked Big Bear, unsure of what the answer is going to be.

"Yes," replied the voice, "It goes up and down."

"AHA!" cried Big Bear. "That means that if I can dig myself into this hole, I am also capable of digging myself out of it?"

"Precisely," said the voice.

"First, I have to understand why I am here before I can understand how I can get myself out of here."

"You have an attitude," continued the voice," and sometimes you only look for what is the best thing for you."

"You make me sound like an opportunist. What does this have to do with me and Little Bear?" asked Big Bear.

"Many things," said the voice. "The two of you only reach a compromise after things have come to a head. You both care about each other and both know that possibly, someday, the two of you will want to have a permanent arrangement. But the compromises tend to be a little one-sided."

"Does this have something to do with wearing watches in the Hundred Pecker Wood?" asked Big Bear.

"That has a lot to do with it, but it is still only part of the problem. It has to do with some of the depth that you are experiencing right now."

"I still don't see the 'pride' in any of this," replied Big Bear, "all I see is a judgment being made and it seems out of my control."

"Control. You used that phrase in the Pool of Despair. Did you learn nothing from that experience? When you were in control the waters were calm. When you let your emotions overcome you, the whirlpool consumed you."

"I am holding my emotions now," replied Big Bear, "and so far it seems to be getting me nowhere."

"Going nowhere - in your case - is better than continuing to go down."

"True," said Big Bear, "But moving towards the surface means I'll have to swallow my pride, or something like that?"

"Something like that," replied the voice.

"And what is the opposite of Pride - Humility?" asked Big Bear.

"Humility is a Goodly Virtue, Pride is a Deadly Sin," said the voice.

"You sound like Shakesbear," said Big Bear, sarcastically.

"You may yet find your answer in Shakesbear, if you look hard enough," replied the voice. "However, words are only words. Many a person has said something merely because it was expected or needed or necessary at the moment. That process alone will not dig you out of the hole you find yourself in."

"That still sounds as though you are judging me," replied Big Bear.

"You will find that we are most harsh when we are judging ourselves. Remember, the Pool of Despair is totally in or out of your control."

Big Bear sat there in silence at the bottom of the well. For a long time he thought about his relationship with Little Bear. Although he was very upset by the events of the past three days and was very unsure about the best way to proceed, he knew that deep inside him he did not hate Little Bear in spite of the events that had occurred. He sat and sat, looking up at the opening above his head, wondering how he was ever going to get himself out of his predicament.

"I'm sorry, Little Bear," began Big Bear, "I'm sorry for all I have done that may have upset you." Suddenly there was a crashing of rock and dirt all around him! "HELP!" cried Big Bear. "What is going on?"

"Oh," replied the voice, rather matter-of-factly "The hole fills itself up quite differently than it empties. I suggest you stand in the center of the hole and let it fall in around you. That way you will not get hit by the falling debris."

"Auugh!" exclaimed Big Bear. "You might have warned me!" He brushed himself off and waited for the dust to settle. He began again: "I'm so sorry, Little Bear, for everything that I have done that I didn't know would upset you." There was a slight tremble. "I didn't know that I was being insensitive." More dirt and rock fell into the hole, and Big Bear discovered that he had risen about three feet higher than he was. "WOW!" he said when the dust had settled once more. The voice did not reply. Big Bear stood there trying to understand what he had done to continue to correct the situation. "Yes," Big Bear admitted, "I can't help but be envious of the fact that my finances are in such poor shape and you seem to be so much better off, Little Bear, and can better afford things when we go out together. I know I have been relying on you, and I apologize. If you feel I have taken advantage of you, well, I guess I have. I will resolve to do better in the future, Little Bear." The ground began to quake and dirt and rocks fell for a long time. Big Bear struggled to keep his balance. When the dirt settled, Big Bear found that he was much closer to the top than he expected to be. "Maybe I was relying on Little Bear more than I thought," thought Big Bear.

The blue sky was still there above him; he could feel the warm sunshine striking his face, but there still was a ways to go before Big Bear would be able to climb out of the hole.

"Little Bear," Big Bear began, "I have always known that you have been hurt and envious of me because I am extroverted and other Bears find me handsome. You yourself have said that I bestow my gifts on those who find me attractive. I do this to make myself feel better. I crave constant attention - you have known this. You knew this at the beginning when we first met. You allowed me the freedom to do this." Big Bear paused, waiting to see if dirt would fall into the hole, or if he would sink back into the ground. There was not even a tremble. Big Bear thought and thought. "I know that I have neglected your feelings at times. I am truly sorry. From now on I promise that I will try to be a better friend."

Suddenly, there was a loud crash and rumbling, and Big Bear found that clouds of dust, dirt and debris surrounded him. He knew that something was happening, but he was still unsure of exactly what. The earth around him was moving so quickly that he could not tell if he was moving up or down. Soon Big Bear realized that he was standing on a mound and that is was moving upwards. Like an elevator, Big Bear moved up the shaft and out of the well! The movement of the earth pushed him upward quickly, and he popped out of the hole like a cork in a bottle!

~

As Big Bear traveled through the air he looked down, expecting to see the landscape where he lived. Instead of the trees and hills he was expecting, the ground was dry and sandy. A dry yellow sky replaced the blue one that had beckoned above him from the depths of the well. The Sun shone bright orange against it. Soon, Big Bear began to fall. "At least the sand will be softer than rocks or trees," he thought. Big Bear hit the ground, hard, and rolled a few times before he stopped. When he sensed that he was no longer moving and had suffered no broken bones, Big Bear opened his eyes and looked around him. All there was to see was hot, dry sand; there wasn't a tree or rock, or any water.

"I'm in a desert," he said, waiting for something to

happen. Nothing happened. "I wonder where 'the voice' is," he pondered, "I suppose it only comes if I ask where I am."

"You are quite right, Big Bear," replied the voice. "Many have found themselves in your same predicament and have never asked the most basic question of all: Where am I?"

"And you just sit around waiting for them to ask the first question?"

"I can't provide an answer if you don't ask a question. Do you remember where I said I am?" asked the voice.

"You said that you are deep within me."

"If that which you seek you cannot find within yourself, you will never find it outside of yourself."

"Well, you are talking to me, so therefore I did ask where I am," replied Big Bear.

"You are in the arid desert of your guilt."

"GUILT? What guilt? What am I guilty of?" demanded Big Bear. "Guilt implies judgment."

"Guilt is a condition," began the voice, 'but some people are good at passing off their guilt onto others, or ignoring their guilt entirely. King Arthur's guilt was borne by Guinevere, according to the legends."

"I'm standing here in a desert and you are making literary allusions," said Big Bear. "The only thing Arthur was guilty of was allowing Camelot to fall into neglect as he neglected himself."

"There are many forms of guilt as well," continued the voice, "Arthur almost destroyed Camelot; then he realized that his knights were fighting his causes, Lancelot carried his honor, Guinevere his guilt, and Mordred his sins, and it roused him into action."

"Excuse me," interjected Big Bear, "I have been through the whirlpool of my despair, and have been almost buried in the well of my pride. Does everything come in threes? It's like I've become a character in a Dickens story."

"And who is making literary allusions now?" asked the voice.

"I am trying to see how all this is supposed to tie together. So far, everything is somehow connected to Little Bear's and my relationship. I drowned in despair; I found out I have an overactive ego. I am still trying to understand what I am guilty of or why I am supposed to feel guilty in this instance. Based on my experiences so far, if I discover and 'admit' my guilt, it will somehow propel me out of this desert. I don't feel I was supposed to be here in the first place."

"Are you in denial?" asked the voice.

"Denial? Denial of <u>what</u>? Guilty of <u>what</u>? I feel as though I am being judged again," said Big Bear.

"And once again, you are showing that you desire the need to be in control," replied the voice.

"Well, this is what you have been telling me all along; you tell me that I am some kind of 'control freak.' You are still judging me, somehow, and I really don't like it!" snapped Big Bear. "Little Bear is out of control. Someone has to stay in control!"

"And what are you feeling now?" asked the voice.

"At least I <u>have</u> feelings; all you are is a disembodied voice."

"Oh-ouch," said the voice "is that that supposed to hurt me?"

"I can't hurt you - you are only a voice."

"Then, what are you feeling?" asked the voice again.

"I felt lost, and then I learned that despair can

swallow you up if you let it. It is one thing to feel loss; it is another to let that loss take over your life," said Big Bear.

"What else?" asked the voice.

"I found that I was not being a good friend because I placed all the emphasis on myself. I learned that unbridled pride feeds on itself but cannot consume itself. When I admitted I needed to become a better friend I was able to go beyond the 'self'," replied Big Bear.

"And now your guilt has brought you here," stated the voice.

"WHAT GUILT? Show me a crime I am guilty of!" demanded Big Bear.

"Why did you cause Little Bear to have a bipolar episode?"

"I caused? What do you mean 'I caused'? I had nothing to do with the triggers for this episode!" yelled Big Bear.

"Sure you did," replied the voice, calmly, "You think your behaviors had nothing to do with this?"

"I may have been neglectful, but neglect does not cause a bipolar episode," stated Big Bear. In the distance there was a faint rumble, barely audible.

"Your neglect started a paranoia reaction. You have been non-supportive and short-tempered."

Big Bear stood up. "Little Bear was under a lot of stress and strain at work. In a job where 'performance' is everything he began to feel that his co-workers were dumping their unwanted students on him, yet he was still expected to maintain a high degree of teaching standards. I alone did not cause this episode to happen. I may have been an inadvertent contributing factor, but this is hardly a cause for guilt. I can correct my wrongs in the future." There was now an obvious rumbling sound coming from the horizon. "What was that rumble?" asked Big Bear.

"Distant storm," replied the voice.

"I can correct my wrongs," began Big Bear again, "but what makes him act this way? So self-destructive! What makes him want to destroy everything - maybe even himself? Do you know? Can you tell me what the answer is?"

"To help him?" asked the voice. "I don't know what the answer is."

"Well, I've got to find the answer," began Big Bear. "You don't know what it's like to watch someone you care about just crumble away, bit by bit, day by day in front of your eyes and stand there, helpless! Caring and loving isn't enough - I thought it was." Tears started to form in Big Bear's eyes. He did not see the dark clouds gathering.

"Sometimes the loving is all you have'" replied the voice.

"I thought I was the answer for his problems," said Big Bear. "I'm afraid of what I saw beginning to happen - within him and within me - because sometimes I hated him! I hate his promises 'to stop' and the watching and the waiting to see it begin again. To come home to him at night and listen to his lies! My heart goes out to him because I deeply believe that somewhere inside all that yelling and reacting that he cares for me, and needs me, too!" It began to mist very quietly, but Big Bear did not notice.

"Love and hate are both very strong human emotions," said the voice. "Sometimes they are separate, but sometimes they go hand in hand; sometimes they are one and the same. Do you care for Little Bear?"

"Of course I care for Little Bear!" cried Big Bear. "I love him - but I hate him, too! I hate him for failing!" Rain had begun to fall.

"Failing? Failing to what?" asked the voice.

"Failing to remember who cares for him - cares about him! How can you forget who your friends are? Who your family is? I hate me because I failed, too!" The storm had built up quickly and thunderbolts were crackling across the horizon. Crying, Big Bear had fallen to his knees and the rain was pouring down over him.

"How did you fail?" asked the voice over the sounds of the storm. "Why do you hate yourself?"

"All during those three days," shouted Big Bear to be heard over the storm, "I tried to be calm, I tried to be reasonable, and Little Bear accused me of horrible things I never did. I thought about all my conversations with you, and realized one thing that you never talked about. The capacity for loving never stops! I hate me for not being able to get through to him in that wild, mixed up state of his mind that no matter what - I am the one person who truly does care for him! That's why I failed! If I could have just gotten through..."

"Maybe you did, maybe you didn't ..." began the voice. The storm was quite violent by now, and winds were rushing about, driving the rain harder and harder into Big Bear's fur.

"And now he's gone! Now I'll never know! And

now I'll never be able to tell him. How much can you love somebody and not tell them? How do you live out the days? How? I failed a friend, I failed as a friend, and now I can't even try to correct the situation! That's why I am a failure and that's why I hate ME!" There was a loud crash of thunder as a lightning bolt lit up the sky.

Big Bear sat bolt upright in bed.

5 - DENOUEMENT

Big Bear went to the theatre to try to get away from his dreams. By some chance of Fate, he went to see a production of 'Macbeth' by William Shakesbear. Not very long into the performance he realized that he had no idea what had prompted him to see this particular play. "This is dreadful!" he thought, "Why did I come here to see this play of *all* plays? Lady Macbeth is going mad and has lost touch with reality. What am I doing here? Why did I come?"

Still, Big Bear stayed at the performance. Lady Macbeth did her sleepwalking scene where she constantly washed her hands and spoke profound nonsense. At the end of the act, Macbeth summons a doctor to try to unwind the mysteries of her behavior:

Macbeth: How does your patient, Doctor?

Doctor: Not so sick, my lord,

As she is troubled by thick-coming fancies

That keep her from her rest.

Macbeth: Cure her of that!

Canst thou not minister to a mind diseased,

Pluck from the memory a rooted sorrow,

Raze out the sweet troubles of the brain,

And with some sweet obvious antidote

Cleanse the stuffed bosom of that perilous stuff

Which weighs upon the heart?

Doctor: Therein the patient must minister to himself.

Big Bear realized then that he was not responsible for what he could not control. Whatever had happened to Little Bear, Little Bear would only get better if he helped himself. That night, much to his relief, Big Bear did not have any more strange dreams.

The next morning he awoke to the ringing of his phone. The Caller Identification did not list a name or number. Big Bear decided to answer it. A small voice asked "Hello? Is that you, Big Bear?"

"Who is this?" asked Big Bear.

"It's Little Bear," the voice replied "I've been in the hospital. After I left your house I went to see my doctor. We agreed that it would be best if I went into the hospital. I am very, very sick."

"How are you feeling?" asked Big Bear tentatively.

"I have a long way to go," he replied. "I am on many medications, and the doctors will not let me drive. I do not like being here, but I have to do this to become better again."

"Are the doctors saying anything about when you will be released?" asked Big Bear.

"Maybe in another two or three weeks," replied Little Bear. "It is very sad to be away from everyone. Can you come to see me when I get better?"

Big Bear thought a long time before he spoke again. He did not want any more hurt feelings between them. "When you get better," he carefully said "I will come to see you and we will talk."

"I understand" replied Little Bear. "Perhaps in a week I will be able to call you again and tell you how I am progressing."

"That will be fine" replied Big Bear. "I will wait until you call me again."

Little Bear stayed at the hospital for two more weeks, taking medications and seeking therapy. Once a week he would call the Big Bear and they would talk about how things were going in their lives. One day Little Bear called to say that the doctors thought that Little Bear could be allowed to go home at night and return to the hospital as a day patient. "Will you come to see me when I get home?" asked Little Bear. "Yes," replied Big Bear "I will come to see you."

Big Bear and Little Bear did see each other. Many things were said, and many things were left unsaid.

. . . .

So they went off together. But wherever they go, and whatever happens to them on the way, somewhere in the world two bears, one Big one and one Little one are walking through the woods together, laughing and joking and wearing their silly bear hats.

6 - IN CONCLUSION

As it was stated in the opening – the fairy-tale ending of Chapter Five <u>did</u> happen – briefly, anyway; but it was not without a few sacrifices along the way. The ending was originally conceived to be a more positive one - having been written a short time after Little Bear started to regain his mental health. This book was clearly intended to be an 'inspiring' story of the triumph of loving rather than the 'cautionary tale' of a flawed relationship's destruction by mental illness that it became. This manuscript sat unfinished and untouched for about twelve years.

Once Little Bear experienced his literal and literary meltdown, Big Bear was faced with many hard choices, one being where to live and the other what would happen to the security from the job that currently employed him. The first question his friends asked him, of course, was if he was going to try to salvage or rebuild what was left of his relationship with Little Bear; most people advised him to take the hospitalizations as hard evidence of past and future problems and to quickly walk away - leaving the relationship, the apartment, and the employment, if necessary. In fact – the term 'the dragons in his head' came from those discussions. In another discussion Big Bear found himself saying to someone: 'It was as though the man I knew had simply melted away and was gone' – and realized he had found the literary device to bridge the diverse sections of the story together.

Big Bear did – in fact - go to see a production of Macbeth during Little Bear's hospitalization; that is not poetic license or a literary device.

Eventually with therapy, time, medications, and evaluation, Little Bear was able to rejoin the rest of his world; even taking up his teaching and performing positions again. Slowly Big Bear and Little Bear were able to rekindle and continue their relationship. Two years later Little Bear purchased a house for the two of them, and Big Bear left his job and moved out-of-state to live with Little Bear. For a period of the next seven years Little Bear's dragons did not return, and the two bears enjoyed such activities such as going abroad with a chorus doing singing tours to Ireland, Scotland, and Switzerland, Little Bear as the accompanist and Big Bear in the baritone section. In accordance with the social and political movements of the time, the Bears became Domestic Partners, and in late 2009 had a Civil Union which would be converted to a marriage in early 2010.

However, in the short span of time between the Civil Union and its conversion to a marriage Big Bear became acutely aware that something was not right with Little Bear and very soon after the marriage was granted a sudden deterioration in Little Bear's mental state brought about a brief institutionalization; the dragons were coming back. Although they did manage to stay together to celebrate their first wedding anniversary, Little Bear's behaviors became more and more erratic. Shortly after the tenth anniversary of the day they met their relationship took an unexpected drastic and traumatic turn, forcing Big Bear to have no other choice but to move out of their house and file for divorce, citing 'irreconcilable differences'. Shortly before the divorce was finalized in 2012, the State declared Little Bear to be incompetent, and made him a Ward of the State. Except for a few brief communications since, Big Bear maintains a restraining order against Little Bear as part of the divorce agreement.

So much for happy endings.

Big Bear

7 – ESSAY – 'HE LOOKED SO SMALL'

(This essay picks up where Chapter Five left off, and is not part of the story. This (and the following essay) should give you an idea of the type of notes that were used to create the fictionalization. Once again – names have been changed.)

~

LB shuffled his way around the corner of the garage to show me where to park. My first reaction was how tiny he appeared. I was about an hour later than I anticipated arriving, having left Connecticut at 2:30 and traffic delays on Rte. 128 caused me to get to Massachusetts after 5:30 p.m. He shuffled over to me and reached up to throw his arms around me, and he seemed as though he had lost height. His beard and his haircut were overgrown. "I'm sorry you had such a horrible trip up, but I'm so glad you're here!"

I had a bag with small Christmas gifts for him, and one

for his parents. "Should I bring my clothes in?" I asked. He replied that he didn't know if we would stay there or not, maybe get a hotel room. He led me into the house. He walked in very small shuffling steps like someone heavily medicated, but his speaking voice was fine. We went into the house. "Oh. Are these Christmas gifts for me? All your gifts are in ____. I can't go get them yet." I replied that it didn't matter. He showed me the room his parents had cleaned up for me, if I had decided to stay. After a two-hour drive that turned into a 3-hour plus ride, I was not about to turn around and leave. "Maybe we should just get a hotel room," he said.

LB's father G came around a corner. "BB, I'm so glad you made the trip," he said, " LB is so glad you came up." Seeing G and LB standing next to each other, you swore that LB was a lot older, and he is all of 3 years older than I am. We all went upstairs. LB decided he needed to make the hotel reservations while G made me some tea. After LB left, G sighed and shook his head. "We just don't know what happened," he said, "but I think LB missed some of his meds. This happened before, you know." I replied I knew about 1996. "In 1992 - also," he added. "He's on a pile of meds - as soon as he takes them tonight he'll go right out."

LB came back and we all had tea and V-8 juice and talked. S, LB's mother was returning from a funeral in Philadelphia, and would not get there until late. We decided to eat and go to the hotel. LB would sit there talking, but his eyelids drooped every now and then.

He's under a whole lot of meds, I thought. No wonder they can't let him drive. Since he had a morning appointment with the doctor, I asked if we really should go to a hotel, but Jed decided he wanted to go, so we went. As we walked to the car, he commented about how he really wants to drive, but he's stuck. He also realizes that he can't drive.

We drove back down the highway a few exits and went to the hotel, with a restaurant attached. After getting the room we went to eat. "I really just want to hold you all night and listen to you talk," he said. We ordered dinner and talked. He showed me the list of meds he is on - a grid printed out at to what he has to take when. It seems like a hell of a lot of meds. At bedtime he has to take at least one of everything, one of them 3 pills. One wonders what is being controlled here. His breathing was very labored. He spoke fine, ate fine, got up and walked around once or twice without any difficulty. But the eyes...cloudy. The face wrinkled and worn. The hands puffy. This man who plays the piano so beautifully.

"So, have you touched a keyboard lately? Other than the lesson you gave last weekend?" He replied that he has played every now and then, but for short times. At the hospital he played a sing-along or two. "Oh, God!" I said, "LB is going to turn into a lounge lizard!" "Hardly!"

We talked delicately around a few issues. I told him about some of the people he said he spoke with or visited with who simply didn't exist. He replied "I must have been REALLY manic during that time." He asked about some of the things that happened because he remembers that we discussed breaking off the relationship. I decided this was neither the time nor place to go into this stuff. He agreed.

We finally went to find the room. It was lovely. We got comfortable and he brought out the couple of gifts he had for me. "Do you want to do a gift exchange now?" Why not? I thought; what difference does it make? LB had coordination problems tearing the paper; I had to help him get started. I gave him many small things. I also gave him a silk tie with a grizzly bear standing in a stream on it. He cried. "This will be my favorite tie of all time," he said.

He wanted to be held; I held him. "This is all I could think about in the hospital, how much I wanted to touch you," he said. He pulled two handfuls of pill bottles out of his luggage and took nine pills. We went to sleep.

We ate breakfast at the hotel. They sat us in the same booth we had occupied the night before. He asked about some of what had happened. I told him it was chronicled, but I did not think he should be reading it. He thought about that and replied that maybe he did not want to read it, ever.

While we were driving back to his parent's house, he asked about the two of us joining my bear club. I replied that I didn't know what would happen if we decided not to stay together, having a joint membership. I figured I had better broach that subject. He thought about it and said that there was still a lot of time, so we didn't have to make any decisions. "I will come back out on the other side of this," he said.

I brought him home. S was there, and greeted me warmly. She had gone out to attend to the funeral arrangements for an uncle and was the only mourner at the church. She was busy getting ready for the family Christmas party this weekend. "I have a gift for you...somewhere," she said. LB got his stuff together and we packed him into his father's truck, and then I left.

****

LB called me a little while ago to see how my return trip home was, and to tell me that they are cutting back on some of his meds. He won't know until next week sometime if he will be allowed to drive. I do not expect to see him again until after Christmas.

{Written December 2002}

Big Bear

8 – ESSAY – 'HE LOOKED BETTER'

It had been about a week and a half since I have seen him. We have spoken on the phone during that time. LB is still taking trips to the outpatient group therapy stuff, and is still not allowed to drive. When I saw him before Christmas we had discussed my driving up again before New Year's. Since that time he seems to be getting out more, and when he called on Saturday from the lobby of some magic show, I thought that he would ask about my coming up. He didn't. I let it slide until Sunday a.m.

I called him on Sunday to see how he was doing. His meds have been slowly changed to a lower dosage, and a couple of them were discontinued. I asked him how he was feeling, and he said 'fine.' He is very antsy about getting his license to drive back. I finally asked him if he'd wanted me to drive up. "Do you really want to come up?" he asked, voice brightening. "I'd have thought you were tired of driving places by now." (Between 12/15 and 12/27 I drove across Connecticut 4 times.) I told him that is he wanted me to come up that I would. He got very happy that he would not have to tag along with his family. We discussed going to see "The Two Towers". I told him I would leave by 2:30 and hoped that I would not get stuck in the massive traffic that I was caught in the last visit. LB decided we could go back to the hotel again, and asked if I had a swim suit small enough for him to wear. I packed two suits and two towels and left for Massachusetts.

This drive was smooth and uneventful, even if it took longer than the time allotted on MapQuest® and I cruised at a high rate of speed. I wanted to get to the house before darkness fell, and I still missed the driveway twice before getting the correct one. On the way LB had called to check my progress and told me that he was practicing Liszt and that he felt a hesitation in his left hand. "At least he is still practicing", I thought. I pulled in the driveway and honked the horn.

LB came out to meet me. "I'm so glad you decided to make the trip," he said. He was not shuffling and seemed to be moving around better. He led me into the house to show me the stuff he had gotten for Christmas from his family. "Oh," he said "I have the gift my parents bought you." I remember that S had mentioned that she had something 'that I had the flair to wear': it was a black silk tie with a bright red Chinese dragon painted on it that she had bought on a trip to China this past summer. It is quite beautiful. I asked LB if they had ever tasted the bizarre jelly (apricot/jalapeño) I had given them. He said they had, and enjoyed it. Shopping bags in hand, we went out to my car and drove to the hotel. Jed said he had checked on start times for LOTR and due to the length of the film it had either an early or a very late start time - however it was being shown in four of the 20 theatres at the complex! It was still early.

We got to the hotel and got our room and checked out the shortest path to the pool. We got into our suits and went down to get in. The pool was indoors in a four-season room, but the pool was NOT heated! It was actually a little too cool in the pool and after a few minutes of walking around we went into the hot tub to warm up. We decided that we should go to dinner early and got dressed and went to the restaurant.

At dinner LB discussed that his meds had been adjusted and he was almost back down to the levels he was taking before the episode started. He was still going to the outpatient sessions but felt that those would probably be ending shortly, too. He really did hope he would be able to get his license back soon; however, his parents did want an evaluation by a doctor before his keys were returned. We ate and talked without realizing what time was passing. It was almost time for the showing to start, and we dropped everything and ran to the car to travel to the movie theatres.

It was a big mall; in fact, with 20 screens you believe that the mall was built around the theatres. By the time I found a parking place and got in and found the theatre, LB had gotten to the line and found out the show was completely sold out but there were tickets available for the 10:30 p.m. showing - of a three-hour nine-minute movie. We decided to buy advance tickets and return. We returned to the restaurant to have dessert.

We decided that I should open my Christmas gifts from him; many small things including some bears, a leather-scented car deodorizer, a bear flag license plate holder, and a bag with a shoulder strap to carry around when I 'don't have pockets.' Since we had finished dinner LB decided to take his after-dinner meds. "Won't they knock you out?" I was more concerned that LB would get antsy and want to walk around during the movie more than his falling asleep during it. After all, I am used to staying up until 2 a.m.

We did see the movie and LB sat there and stayed awake for the entire picture. What a magnificent movie! Can't believe I have to wait another year to see the final film. We went back to the hotel and gave a wake-up call; we ate breakfast the next morning and I drove LB back to his parent's house, and returned home.

✻✻✻✻✻✻✻✻✻✻✻✻✻✻✻

Two hours later I was back home, and shortly thereafter LB called me to say that he had seen the doctors who decided he did not need to continue with the outpatient therapy. They also were returning his car keys to him. I was more concerned that LB was getting his keys back with New Year's Eve around the corner and after not dealing with traffic for a month, now being caught in holiday crowds. He did spend New Years' Eve at a club, has since driven to his home to give a private piano lesson, and had returned to his school office to catch up on everything he needs to.

{Written January 2003}

ABOUT THE AUTHOR

BIG BEAR is a pen name; the author has chosen to remain unidentified.

www.ingramcontent.com/pod-product-compliance
Lightning Source LLC
Chambersburg PA
CBHW050503290526
45786CB00006B/2415